P9-CFM-566

Property of NCS Library

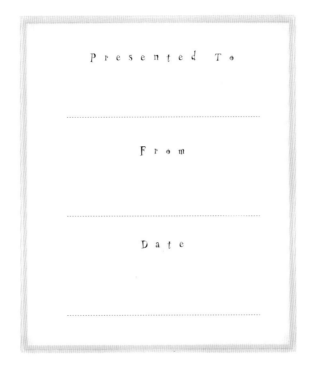

Presented To

........................................

From

........................................

Date

........................................

BETHANY
BACKYARD
www.bethanyhouse.com

*Look What You Made, God!*
Text © 2002 by Elspeth Campbell Murphy
Illustrations © 2002 by Bethany House Publishers
Design and production by Lookout Design Group, Inc. (www.lookoutdesign.com)

Unless otherwise identified, scripture quotations are from the HOLY BIBLE, NEW INTERNATIONAL
VERSION®. Copyright © 1973, 1978, 1984 by International Bible Society. Used by permission of Zondervan
Publishing House. All rights reserved. The "NIV" and "New International Version" trademarks are registered
in the United States Patent and Trademark Office by International Bible Society. Use of either trademark
requires the permission of International Bible Society.

Scripture quotations identified ICB are from the *International Children's Bible, New Century Version*, copyright
© 1986, 1988 by Word Publishing, Dallas, Texas 75039. Used by permission.

Scripture quotations identified TEV are from the Bible in Today's English Version (*Good News Bible*).
Copyright © American Bible Society 1966, 1971, 1976, 1992.

All rights reserved. No part of this publication may be reproduced, stored in a retrieval system, or transmitted
in any form or by any means—electronic, mechanical, photocopying, recording, or otherwise—without
the prior written permission of the publisher and copyright owners.

Published by Bethany House Publishers
A Ministry of Bethany Fellowship International
11400 Hampshire Avenue South
Bloomington, Minnesota 55438
www.bethanyhouse.com

Printed in China.

Library of Congress Cataloging-in-Publication data applied for.

Dear Grown-up,

The young child's response to creation is up close and personal. And something happens for us when we look at God's world through a young child's imaginative eyes: Our own faith is freshened.

That's why the Scripture verses are included in this book—for your own meditation. For example, in one prayer-poem the child delights in the ants who gather around a drop from his ice cream cone. And the accompanying verses (Psalm 104:27–28) remind us as adults that we, too, are created by God and sustained by his grace.

So share this book and God's world with your young child. And may God richly bless you both!

Elspeth Campbell Murphy

*Praise the Lord from the earth*

*. . . you mountains and all hills*

*. . . for his name . . . is above*

*the earth and the heavens.*

PSALM 148:7a, 9a, 13b

# Long Way Down

Rolling,

Rolling,

Rolling,

Wheeee!

The hill reached up and tickled me!

The hill and I are happy that

You made this world

And it isn't

Flat.

*How great is the love the*

*Father has lavished on*

*us, that we should be*

*called children of God!*

*And that is what we are!*

1 JOHN 3:1a

# Hey, Kids!

We're kind of confused at the

petting zoo, God,

And I'll tell you why we are.

Because what if Daddy says,

"Time to go, kids"—

And the baby goats jump in the car?

# Windy Day

"*The wind blows wherever it pleases. You hear its sound, but you cannot tell where it comes from or where it is going. So it is with everyone born of the Spirit.*"

JOHN 3:8

The wind and I were playing, God.
But sometimes he plays too rough.
He blew so hard, he knocked
     me down.
So I said, "That's enough."

I went in the house without him.
He rattled the windows and door.
But I just said, "Unless you behave,
I'm not going to play anymore."

Well, he must have been lonely
     without me,
Because he later came back as a breeze.
He begged me to come out and
     play again.
What else could I do? He said please.

*"Are not five sparrows*

*sold for two pennies?*

*Yet not one of them is*

*forgotten by God.*

*Indeed, the very hairs*

*of your head are all*

*numbered. Don't be afraid;*

*you are worth more*

*than many sparrows."*

LUKE 12: 6–7

# Sparrow Talk

My yard must be a playground for birds—

The sparrows all crowd there together.

They hop and they chirp

And they stir up the dirt

When they flap their little brown feathers.

They hop and they flap,

They won't take a nap,

And they make so much noise when

   they're playing.

I listen as hard as I can to them, God—

I'm glad *you* understand what they're saying!

*All this took place to fulfill
what the Lord had said
through the prophet:
"The virgin will be with
child and will give birth to
a son, and they will call him
Immanuel"—which means,
"God with us."*

# Mmmmmmmmmm!

I *love* this tree!

It's called a pine.

And this is a favorite place of mine.

Because

Even on any old day of the year—

Mmmmmmmmmm—

It smells like *Christmas* here!

*These all look to you to give them their food at the proper time. When you give it to them, they gather it up; when you open your hand, they are satisfied with good things.*

PSALM 104: 27–28

# Plop!

A little drop dripped

From my ice cream cone

And suddenly—

I wasn't alone.

As soon as that drop

Went *plop!* on the ground,

Ants came running from all around.

Ants from here,

Ants from there,

Ants and their cousins from everywhere!

Do little ants know, God,

That food comes from you?

Surprise, you guys!

You got ice cream, too.

*"I [the Lord] am the one*

*who made the beaches to*

*be a border for the sea."*

JEREMIAH 5:22b (ICB)

# At the Beach

You know what, God?

At the beach

The sand is hot hot hot—

But brrrrr!

The water is not not not!

*Nothing in all creation is*

*hidden from God's sight.*

HEBREWS 4:13a

# Hide and Seek

Guess what, God.

My goldfish

Played a trick on me.

She thought that I

Would never see

Her in the grasses

Where she hid.

At first I didn't.

Then I did.

*"Consider how the lilies grow.*

*They do not labor or spin.*

*Yet I tell you, not even*

*Solomon in all his splendor*

*was dressed like one of these."*

LUKE 12:27

# Flower Beds

Today we planted tulips, God.

    I told them,

      "Don't worry about a thing.

      Just settle down for a nice, long nap.

      And God will call you

      When it's spring."

# Chipmunk

*In his hand are the deep*

*places of the earth.*

PSALM 95:4a (KJV)

"Oh, look!

A chipmunk!"

"Where? Where?"

"A little chipmunk!

Over there!

See him scamper?

See him scurry?"

"Where is he going in such a hurry?"

"Into his tunnel, warm and deep,

to curl in a ball

and go to sleep."

A little blur

of stripey fur.

Did we see him?

We're not sure. . . .

# Cozy Cat

*The Lord blesses his people*

*with peace.*

PSALM 29:11b

The cat
looked around
for a place to nap
and chose—
*my lap!*

The cat
snuggled down
when I stroked her fur
and began—
*to purr!*

Cuddled up
with a cozy cat.
What makes you feel
more special
than that?

*Sing for joy to the Lord,*

*all the earth; praise him*

*with songs and shouts of joy!*

PSALM 98:4 (TEV)

# Happy Dog

My dog can't talk, God,

As you know.

But he wants to thank you

For the *snow!*

Snow as far as we can see!

It was as if he said to me:

"SNOW!

SNOW!

SNOW!

SNOW!

OH BOY OH BOY OH BOY!

*LET'S GO!*"

# City Horse

There's a lot to see
In the city, of course,
But I *didn't* expect
To see a *horse*!

With a policeman riding
Way up high,
A big brown horse
Came clopping by.

And all the children
Wanted to pet him—
And the horse you made
Was *glad* to let them!

Yes, that's one thing, God,
I think I should mention.
Your city horse got
A *lot* of attention!

I praise you because

I am fearfully and

wonderfully made;

your works are wonderful,

I know that full well.

PSALM 139:14

# Little Baby

A baby!
A baby!
Ooo, let me see.
Isn't he precious, God?
Isn't he sweet?

Tiny pink tongue,
Buttony nose,
*Teensiest* fingernails,
Bitsiest toes.

You know why I'm glad
There's a baby among us?
It's because
Next to *him*—
*I* look HUMONGOUS!

*"As long as the earth endures, seedtime and harvest, cold and heat,*

*summer and winter, day and night will never cease."*

GENESIS 8:22